This book belongs to

_____

GUS the Gassy Ghost

By Humor Heals Us

My name is Gus and I'm a ghost.
Haunting houses is what I **love** most.

I have a skill that other ghosts don't.
I have very bad gas. It helps me to float.

People get scared and run here and there,
Holding their **noses** and racing down the stairs.

There are vampires, witches, werewolves, and ghouls.
Monsters and zombies that are very cool.

The fact that I'm a **spook**, a spirit, or a ghost
Doesn't seem to scare people, at least not most.

It is my **sneaky** farts that terrify them.
They can't see them coming, so they never know when.

Zombies eat hearts and vampires suck blood.
I release stinky gas that **engulfs** like a flood.

I am known as Gus the ghost with the gas.
Some think I am rude and a little bit **crass**.

I do what I must. It's my job to **alarm**.
Although I don't mean little kids any harm.

People book me for parties through the site "Spooks for Hire."
My farts are an **extra** that's popular with the buyer.

I went with some monsters, all good friends of mine.
A house needed **haunting**. It sounded really fine.

We went through the house finding places to hide.
Some hid in the rooms and others outside.

The vampire took the attic, preparing for scares,
While a skeleton **relaxed** on one of the chairs.

The zombie was outside behind a big tree.
That just left three of us, two witches and me.

The other sat playing with her black cat on the **stairs**,
While I floated around farting. A bit here and a bit there.

Some children came up to the door,
But their knocks were **ignored**.

They tried the doorknob and it turned with a squeak,
So they **pushed** the door open and inside did peek.

The zombie was **furious** he'd just been ignored,
But he didn't realize he'd left his arm on the door.

My friends' attempts to frighten had no effect,
So it was my turn to try. I thought, what the heck!

That made me quite angry, so I let go a fart.
BOOM! That could shake anyone's heart!

Well, they coughed and they spluttered, and ran for fresh air. Monsters couldn't do it, but my farts really **scared**.

Follow us on FB and IG @humorhealsus
To vote on new title names and freebies, visit
us at humorhealsus.com for more information.

 @humorhealsus   f @humorhealsus

Made in the USA
Middletown, DE
11 September 2022

10242200R00022